From the Outside Looking In

The Poetic Journey Continues

B.V. Smith

To order additional copies of this book, contact:
Xlibris Corporation
1-888-795-4274
www.Xlibris.com
Orders@Xlibris.com
57179

Contents

Dedicated To

My children
Nyeta and Donovan
My grandchildren
Bryce, Karma and Gabriella
"I Love You More"

Acknowledgements

First and most of all, I thank GOD for this gift. Lots of love and thanks to my daughter, Nyeta and my son-in-law, Kwabena, my son Donovan and his friend Magda, my forever friend Michael, my brother, Douglas and my sisters Gail and Diane.

Special thanks to Dan Mclean, Alice Cannon, John Neal, Willie and Bobbie Jennings for believing in me. Many thanks to Latifa Saleem, Paulette Barrett and Lori Coppola for your positive insight and well wishes.

Heartfelt thanks to all my airline co-workers and friends. Thank you Mr. James Crawley for your clerical assistance.

Much gratitude to my close friends, Michelle Roberts, Dottie Marks, Dawn McLean-Everitt, Chris Turner, Emma Brown, Jessie Wright, Greg and Tasha Spieghts for all your encouragement.

Many, many thanks to the publishing company, Xlibris.

Barbara V. Smith

I Love To Write

I love to write about good times and laughter
Sunshine and the morning after
I write about being held by your lover
All through the night
At a place in time where happiness feels right

I've tried to capture the emotional bliss of ecstasy
Intermittently dusted with fantasies
Aiming to stress the importance of life and family
A cool breeze, snowflakes or autumn leaves.
I write about *Love*.

I've penned many verses on pain
With raw reality
Some words speak of a good life and peace of mind
Cradled in harmony.
I've reached deep within the wholeness of me
Searching and questioning everything
Needing to write about universal love and hate
Including spiritual growth and the human race
Optimistically wanting to change a few wrongs to right
I expressed hope, even when there was strife.
I write about *Survival*.

Creative forces flow smoothly in the stillness of the eve.
When the moon and stars shine bright
I write with ease
Some phrases are bursting with strength and motivation
As the pen quickly glides across the page
Interpreting the imagination
Striving to write a true work of art
Producing poetic stories that touch many hearts
I write about *Forgiveness*

I Love To Write

Desire

A Lover's Quarrel

We always resolved
Misunderstandings between us
Before going our separate ways.
We talk it out, walk it out
Laugh it away or sex it away
Why not this time?

The other day we parted
Without a hug or kiss
As if neither one of us wanted to stay
Usually, we can not resist.

Since that day there's been only silence
Our intimate times together
Are sincerely missed
This awful aching inside of me
Isn't just emotional
It's also very physical.

These feelings go deep
Down to my core
I hurt in places within my being
That I've never felt pain before.

We're both too stubborn to admit
The power of our love and trust
Please, let's forgive
Let's discuss
Whatever it is or whatever it takes
To rectify, clarify and correct
This mistake.

As lovers, as best friends
Can't we solve this problem?
Then begin again.

I need us to be
The way we were
Happily and Unselfishly

In Love

The Pleasure Zone

Take it easy, Lover
Not so fast
Make this erotic
journey last.
Long enough to make
our bodies tingle
Hot enough to sweat
as we mingle.

Slow it down, Baby
I know you're ready
Keep the flow steady
So we can savor
The juicy flavors
of a sensational treat
That is Oh! So sweet.

Ride with me, Honey
In and out
of the Pleasure Zone
Exciting and sensual
With a spell of its own
Sharing an insatiable appetite
Fulfilling our desires
Just right!

Hold on, my Darling
Let's explore
an intimate adventure
with a climax and more.
Passionate moans
of rhythm in motion
Ultimately achieving
Satisfaction.

Whatever your pleasure
Let it be known
It's very accommodating
Inside the Zone!

Still

I wanted to spend each day
Being loved by you
Looking forward to
Your smile
Your smell
Especially your touch

At times it was difficult to love you
Because it hurts too much.
Though time has erased from my memory
The taste of your lips
My heart and body are still curious
About the passion in your kiss.

When I let myself
Think back and feel.
I must admit
"I will always love you"
After all these years
That love is **STILL** real.

The Ultimate Climax

Those deep dark rooms
In the mansion of our desires
The ultimate climax
Climbs higher and higher.
Exploding like a giant burst of energy
Soaring higher and deeper within me.

So naturally free and smooth flowing
While fantasying the aura starts glowing
Sweet mother nature awaiting her cue.
Bringing you into me and me into you.

Entwined Emotions
Speak the body language
Rejoicing with the pleasures of sensation
A Passionate fragrance of the soul will transpire
As the ultimate climate
Climbs higher and higher.

United

(Search No More)

We share our days and years
Our hearts and fears
We share our problems and our bed
Our friends and the roof over our heads
We share the car keys
The sun, rain and summer breeze.

We share our monies and our bills
Our religion and our ills
We share our love and happiness
Our failures and success
We share the bathroom shower
The seconds, minutes and daily hours.

We share our laughter and mood swings
Our marriage complete with the rings
Since the day we both said "I Do"
I look forward to the future with you.

Special

Angela

"An Angel On Earth"

We're all here to celebrate the Angela we know and love
On her twenty-first birthday
We're celebrating
Her smile
Her beauty
Her style
Her love of music and travel
Her youthfulness and her Libra ways.

Angela, your joyful spirit tugs at our heartstrings
Penetrating our souls.
Reminding us of happier times
Your loved ones are here by your side
You're always in our thoughts and prayers
Each day.

Give us a smile!! Open your eyes!!

Dance Angela Dance!
To the rhythmic songs of life, of love, of joy
Let your hair sway to each beat
Listen to the many sounds that vibrate around you
Stimulating your mind and arousing your spirit.

We are here to celebrate you, Angela
A very vibrant, gifted and sweet individual.
"An Angel On Earth"

So Dance Angela
Move your feet to the beat of life!
Happy 21st Birthday.

You're The One (for me)

I knew from the start
That you would steal my heart
I tried to fight the feeling
My emotions hit the ceiling
The passion runs deep
Straight to my soul
What's happening to me?
I'm losing control

No matter what I do
My thoughts are of you
Even though you never say
That you feel the same way
My heart starts to pound
Whenever you're around
All you have to do is smile
My imagination goes wild.

The sound of your voice
Always excites me
While admiring your body
I long for intimacy
My devotion is strong
I won't be untrue
I've loved you too long
Nothing is right without you

Your sensuous eyes
See who I am inside
We feel so much for each other
Be more than a friend
Be my lover.
Some nights I can't sleep
I'm alone between the sheets
Wanting you here with me
Instead of a love fantasy

Can't you feel the affect
You're having on me?
I'm no longer afraid to say
"I Love You"
You're the one for me
Undoubtedly

Inside Out

Numerous valleys
Mountains and burned bridges
Progression and some standstills
Lots of laughs
Mixed with tears
Joy and sorrow

It's been a long
Life-changing journey
Traveling the pathways together
Hand in hand
Touching our spirits
Linking two souls

We look deep
We love unconditionally
As soulmates do
You see me
I see you

From the Inside Out

I Love You

I love you from the beginning to the end
Of every love song
I love you the way togetherness makes us feel
That we belong
I love you as the dawn overpowers the night
I love you the way darkness respects the light
I love how you make love to me
The way you do
I love you like stars dancing
Around the moon.

I love you like the many temptations
Of forbidden fruit
I love you the way fashion models strut
In designer suits
I love you the way a rainbow paints its colors
Across the sky
I love you like the wingspan of an eagle
As it flies
I love you in every language spoken
Throughout the world
I love you like the taste of chocolate
With vanilla ice cream swirled.

I love you the way ocean waves
Kiss the sea shores
I love you with all my heart
And much, much more.

Happy Valentine's Day

Together Again

Could it be
I lied to me
Many years ago
When we both let go?

We took back our vows and walked away
Living our lives apart
I buried all the pain I felt
Far behind my aching heart

Now we've come full circle
As we stand here face to face
Gazing into each others eyes
In this secluded place

Could it be
That finally
It's our time to be
Together, you and me?

Are we getting a second chance?
At true love from the heart
For better not for worse
Til death us do part.

Starting with romance
Enjoying who we are now
As we rekindle passion's fire
Maybe later renew our vows

Believing we will do better
Now that we're wiser
This time around
I'm grateful for the opportunity
To use the knowledge we've found

Could it be
Destiny?
Our love lived on
So we could be
Together again.

Especially For You, Mother

Mother, your nurturing
Inspiration and endless love
Has made me a better person
Your hard work and sacrifice
Afforded me various opportunities
Thank you for all the support

We did not always agree
Still, you were honest and fair
Letting me make my own
Choices and mistakes
While offering words of wisdom

For caring and sharing
For happiness and good times
Mostly for the love you give
Whole-heartedly

Enjoy every moment of this day

Happy Mother's Day

Sky Gypsy

Just Call me the "Sky Gypsy"
Such fun I am having
Worldwide traveling
Born to fly, high in the sky
Different places
Colored by many faces
What an education
While taking a vacation.

Planning my itinerary
How many bags can I carry?
Seated in a plan
Sunshine or rain
From take off to landing
The crew is outstanding
Hope there are no delays
Must reach my destination today.

The beautiful sand and sights
The romantic Caribbean nights
First class, business class and coach
In and out of airports coast to coast
Filled with global curiosity
Both domestic and internationally.

There is very little to compare
Soaring 35,000 feet in the air
I am off to Las Vegas next week
May I have a window seat?
No need denying my love of flying
Just call me the "Sky Gypsy."

More Than A Friend

Knowing I can call upon you
At anytime, is a relief
There's nothing we can't talk about
You never let me down
Your advice is invaluable
For we share a special love.

I've known you most of my life
Our friendship has passed
The test of time
Though we've had disagreements
I can't recall ever having an argument.
You've earned my trust
Respect and love
You're more than a friend
You're family.

Just For You

All my life
There's been a special place in my heart
Just for you
When we talk and spend time together
Exchanging laughs, secrets or tears
I feel surrounded by your love
You are truly a blessing to me.

Your words of encouragement and tough love
Keep me strong
When I feel weak and burdened
Thank you, for always being there for me
Whatever the situation.

The spiritual bond we share
Has bridged the distance between us
Keeping us close

Don't ever doubt
How special you are to me
Or
How much "I love you"
Your inner beauty
Shines through for all to see.

I wish you many Blessings
Peace and great Happiness
I will love you
All my life

(Your Sister)

Life Happens

Live Life

If you ever have a brush with death
Or get close enough to smell its breath
Not easily will you ever forget
Having come so close with no regret

Not being taken away
In the twinkle of an eye
You shiver at the thought
"This time it passed me by"

If you ever cross death's path
Your heart might start beating fast
Dying isn't something you want to do
Yet, it's inevitable
One day death will come for you

Appreciate the precious gift of Life
It's a blessing, so celebrate each day
At any uncertain moment
Your life could be taken away

Lost and Found

I've questioned fate many times in my life
Trying to avoid extra pain and strife
Taking necessary chances
While gambling at will
Toying with destiny to chase a thrill.

Traveling through a mystical maze
As I journey into self
Having occasional second thoughts
"Have I forgotten something else?"

Going through life experimenting
Observing and comprehending
For some it takes longer
To find their direction
Searching for the right form of expression.

Sooner or later, we must all pay our dues
Finding ourselves both
The wise and the fool
Achieving self-awareness
Is an asset in the game
For some things must change
In order to remain the same.

You lose and you find
It all relates to space and time
The reality of it all you see
Is, I finally, finally found me.

Good Luck In Your Search For Self

If You Love Him

The echo of your voice
Remains in your son's mind
His loving heart still wants
to know you better

Maintaining a level of forgiveness
He occasionally asks
"Where is my father?"
"I must find my father."

There are questions that warrant
Seeing the look in your eyes
Things he needs to know about you
To better understand himself.

If you love him
Help him find
The missing pieces of his life
Labeled: Dad

He seeks closure from
The uncertainties of the past
That will set him free
To move on.

Acceptance

Maybe,
If you took the time
To know me
I wouldn't appear to be
such a mystery.

Respect and accept me
For who I am
Bond with me
Love me unconditionally.

Do you love what you see
When you look at me?
Are my wants and needs
Important to you,
As yours are to me?

Does being with you mean
The sacrifice will be me?
Lets search within us
For acceptance of our individuality.

Please stop,
Comparing me to others
If I am not
Who you want and love
Then let me go.

For I can only be
Me!

Astral Projection

In dreams we travel without boundaries
Surfing the spiritual realms
Exploring the beyond
Connecting to the hereafter

Quickly drifting into another dimension
Willing ourselves anywhere at anytime
Words are not needed
For the mind telepathically communicates
To the spirit of the being

Experiencing another life
Another world, within our dreams

Temporarily Out Of Order

My teary eyes reflect
Much disappointment
I'm tired of being angry
Too angry to forgive

The sadness won't let me forget
Prayer helps me bear the pain
Temporarily weakened
By the shock of it
As time passes I will heal

The sunshine in my smile
Will return
Soon, I'll be happy again!

Father Where Art Thou?

Dear Dad,

I'm a young man now
I hope it's not too late for us.

As a child, I prayed day and night
That you would comeback.
To be with me
To play with me
To help me, become a man.

As a young boy, I wanted an occasional embrace
With some fatherly advice
As I ventured out
Into the world each day.

I didn't just need a father figure
I needed you, My Father.

There's no way to match my mother's love
Yet, living my life without your love
Left an empty place deep within me
That only you can fill.

Do you love me, dad?
Do you think we could begin again,
Right now?
As men
As friends
As father and son?

R.S.V.P.
I'll be waiting

Your Son

It's No Fun

Is There something I can do?
Maybe make some chicken soup
Read you a story
Or sit and chat with you

Arrange fresh flowers in a vase
Perhaps tell a joke or two
Hold your hand
Or fluff the bed pillows for you.

I'll bring some cheerful balloons
We can watch your favorite cartoons
It's no fun being sick
So please, Get Well Quick

Farewell

Trust

Trust me,
I am your friend
Confide in me
Your darkest secrets.
Love me deeply
I'll be there for you
With no regrets.

I don't believe you
The truth is in your eyes
You camouflage your true feelings
With a chuckle and a smile.

You give the impression
You're happy for me
But, you're not sincere
It's envy, designed to
Deny your own fear.

Your honesty is interpreted
As unable to find
"The real deal" lies hidden
Within a state of mind.

I have forgiven and tried to forget
Still you have not changed, yet.
You say, you don't realize
How much you have lied.

Trust must be earned
The truth must be learned
Love needs room to grow
Friends come and go.

Today I have one less friend
Trust Me!

Until Today

In the past
>   I foolishly believed
>>   You were loving me
>>>   In your own style

I haven't felt
>   Loved by you
>>   In an extremely
>>>   Long while

Until today
>   Thinking there was hope
>>   I repeatedly tried
>>>   To "fix" us

There's so much frustration
>   Very little communication
>>   Or trust

Argumentative, judgmental
>   So very negative
>>   This is no way
>>>   For partners to live

I understand you now
You don't give a . . . .
No way
No how

After careful evaluation
Of my self worth
I feel like
I'm experiencing a new birth

Therefore,
I can't love you anymore
This should not come
As a surprise
So, don't you dare
Ask me
"Why?"

Dream On

You used to like
Awakening from a deep sleep
To the soft sultry sounds of my voice
Now, you're annoyed by
The ringing of the phone
Sleep, uninterrupted is your choice.

You said, you would answer my calls
No matter what, when or where
Surely long distance communication
Isn't the same as me being there.

How can I possibly compete
Miles and miles away?
With whoever is lying beside you
Through the night and into your day.

You say, "You are special"
Please stay in my life
"I love you and I want you"
I just don't need a wife.

We both have too much time in between
Causing complexity
A good relationship is built on trust
This arrangement doesn't work for me

So, to you I say
"I love you" and "I'll miss you"
C'est la vie *(such is life)*

Soon

(Some words cut deep—The scars can last forever)
One day soon
I will not shed a tear
Those painful words
I will no longer hear
No matter what
You say or do
One day soon
I will stop loving you.

When that day comes
I shall walk away
I need to be loved
In a better way
Those harsh words
Will no longer penetrate my heart

One day soon
When we are apart
The hurting will stop

The Last Chapter

We pretend
We're in love
Speaking fondly
Of one another
To family and friends
Giving occasional
false hugs and effortless kisses.

Behind closed doors
We must face reality
There's still love between us
Yet, we are not in love.

At certain moments
Our hearts remember
What we've shared
We stare at one another briefly
Then exchange phony smiles
How did we let this happen?

As we approach
The last chapter
Of our love story
Can we still save *us*?

Crazy

Don't tell me I'm crazy
Because I found out
Just get your belongings
It's over!
Get out!
We are strangers
Living within these walls
Secrets and betrayal
Walk the halls

Is it craziness
That has broken my heart?
Or is it your lies
That have driven us apart?

The pain I'm feeling
Is not insanity
It's love gone bad
Crying inside of me.

You call me unstable
Telling me "it's all in my mind"
Well, the thrills are gone
Leaving only lost love behind
Along with forgotten vows and
The broken promises
You made to me.

Crazy in love with you
Is what I used to be
Now all I want
Is to be set free!

The End

We've come as far
As we can together
We're at a crossroad
In this relationship.
We've grown apart
We're moving in different directions

No longer feeling the passion
In our souls
Or the beat of love
In our hearts
Sharing our lives
Is not a priority
There have been too many tears
Over the years
Caused by heartache.

Our partnership has dissolved.
Though numbed by this realization
Still, we wish each other
Happiness and a blessed life
Maybe we can salvage
Some desirable memories
Allowing our positive energies to exist.

Feelings of resentment
Are creeping in.
We have finally
Reached the end.
It's time
To say
Good-bye

Faith

I Am Not Alone

I can't deal with you all by myself
But, I know someone who can
He will bring you to your knees
He will make you understand

I can't deal with you all by myself
But, I know someone who can
He knew the solution to the problem
Before it even began

If you're thankful for your blessings
Why are you causing others pain?
There is a time for all things
You can be born again

I can't deal with you all by myself
But, I know someone who can
He will humble you before him
For you are only human

I can't deal with you all by myself
But, I know someone who can
He can part a river or move a mountain
And breathe life into every man/woman

Step out on faith and the strength will come
For I know someone who cares
Fear no evil, fear no one
He always answers prayer.

R.I.P.

We knew this day would come
It was seen from afar
Now it's here and all around us
Heavy on our hearts.

We feel your presence
So happy and so giving
Can't go with you this time
We must stay here
Among the living.

Gone but forever remembered
We miss you "Brother Dear"
Take our love with you to heaven
One day we will see you there.

In memory of Albert (Tookie) Floyd

Going Home

There's a bright light
In the middle of darkness.
A distant voice calls your name
Only you can hear it.
You don't want to leave, but
Your life's work here is done
Relax and let go of the flesh.

You can sing with angels
As you walk around heaven
The place our Lord has prepared.
You'll tire no more.
Embrace the loved ones
Already passed on
Relax and let go of this world

Praise Him

Lord, thank you for lifting me up
Holding me close
Blessing me

Lord, thank you for your Mercy
Deliverance from evil
For comforting me

Lord, thank you for your Peace
I feel your presence
My fears disappear
Each time I call
You answer prayer

Lord, thank you for your Grace
The Holy Spirit
Repentance and Forgiveness

Lord, thank you for your Miracles
Your Angels
Prophets and Saints

Lord, thank you for your Son, Jesus
He shed his blood
For our salvation

Lord, thank you for your Love
The breath of life
The precious gift of children and family
My mate and close friendships

Lord, thank you for all
The material things
You allow me to possess

Thank you for loving me more
Than I could ever love myself
To you, I give all Praise

Life Lessons

Father, I thank you
For all my life lessons
For your many
Miracles and blessings
Please forgive me, I pray
If I fail to pass
My life lesson today.

NOTES

NOTES

NOTES

....

....

....

....

....

....

....

....

....

....

....

....

....

....

NOTES

NOTES

....

....

....

....

....

....

....

....

....

....

....

....

....

....

NOTES

NOTES

NOTES

NOTES

NOTES